BIG FEELINGS

T0347703

Dedicated to Mikah,
my daughter, and her big
beautiful feelings. I love you
with my whole heart.

 Find me on every page!

REBEKAH BALLAGH

BIG FEELINGS

And what they tell us

ALLEN&UNWIN
SYDNEY·MELBOURNE·AUCKLAND·LONDON

Emotions are messages from your heart,
they tell you what you need.
Some of them are BIG feelings,
and some are very small indeed.

Imagine your feelings as clouds, floating in the sky.
Sometimes dark and stormy,
sometimes calm and bright.

Happy feelings, worried ones, mad or glum and blue.
Listen to each feeling,
sent here to help you.

Mikah feels so sad,
tears are rolling down her face.
She's looked for Cuddly everywhere,
but Cuddly's gone without a trace.

"It's okay," says Nana,
"to feel sad and have a cry."
She snuggles Mikah in a hug
beside the cosy fire.

Mikah's chin begins to quiver,
she thinks it's all gone wrong.
But she knows just what to do,
she won't be sad for long.

Feeling sad lets Mikah know
she needs kindness and self-care,
a hug from someone special
and a willing listening ear.

It helps her to imagine
a calm and happy place,
and remember all the lovely things
that make her feel she's safe.

Chloe's feeling angry,
she yells and slams the door.
Her brother calls her Cranky Croc
as she stomps across the floor.

Anger lets Chloe know
something hasn't gone her way.
It sometimes tells her she is sad
beneath that big display.

Chloe knows just what to do
to let her anger out.
She jumps, throws pillows at the wall,
or breathes and slowly counts.

It's okay to feel mad and angry,
it helps to name it too.
Just safely let your anger out,
for the people around you.

Charlie feels so anxious,
his worries pop up like bubbles.

He's scared of reading
to the class . . .

. . . of monsters . . .

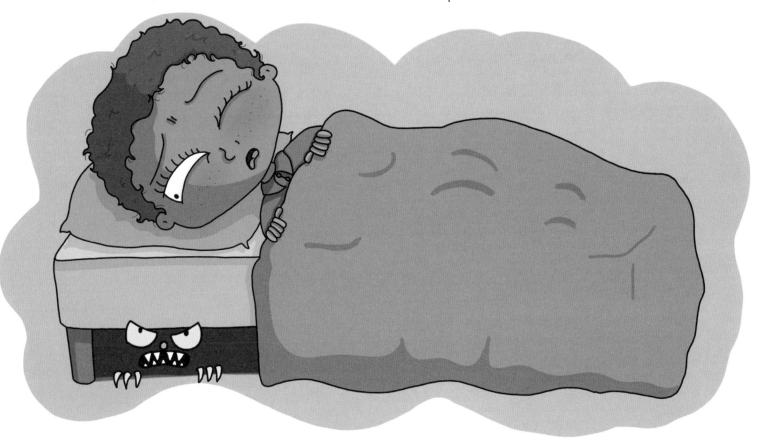

. . . and getting in trouble!

Anxiety makes Charlie's tummy sink,
he feels a little funny.
But it's normal to notice things like that
when you're feeling worried.

"Worry helps me
think and plan
and get myself prepared."

Things usually turn out better
than Charlie might have feared.

Breathing slowly helps,
and talking to his teddies.
Now Charlie's feeling brave again,
his heart is calm and steady.

When Henry is feeling kind,
his heart tells him to help others.
He lends a hand, plays nice and fair . . .

. . . and saves poor bees from puddles.

'Treat others how you want to be treated',
that is Henry's aim.

A heart that's filled with kindness
makes you feel all warm inside.
You'll fill the world with love,
and your heart will burst with pride.

Albie feels content,
everything seems to be all right.

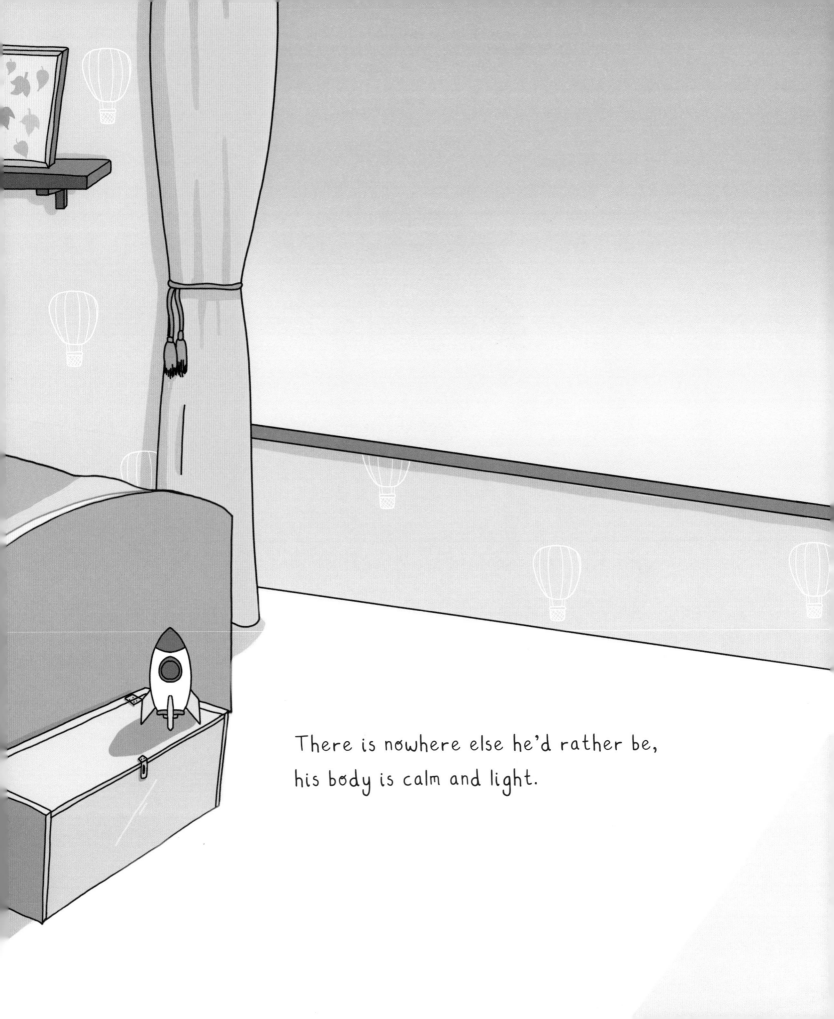

There is nowhere else he'd rather be,
his body is calm and light.

Feeling calm means Albie's mind
is relaxed and free from worry.
It reminds him to be grateful,
to breathe deep and not to hurry.

When Cora is feeling happy,
everyone can tell.
She laughs and leaps about the house,
and jumps for joy as well.

Cora feels happy
when she's with her friends,
or eating ice cream in a cone,
or playing dinosaur pretend.

At times when she is feeling down,
Cora knows just what to do.
She remembers all the lovely things in life . . .

and her heart fills with gratitude.

Izzy is scared of spiders,
the dark and starting school.
Her mouth feels dry, her mind is racing,
her legs are wobbly too!

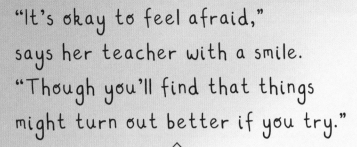

"It's okay to feel afraid,"
says her teacher with a smile.
"Though you'll find that things
might turn out better if you try."

Izzy feels brave again when she thinks of something else.

Now Izzy knows just what to do, she turns on her night light.
When you breathe in deep and face your fears,
most things turn out all right.

Angus feels let down,
his heart is disappointed.
It's raining this morning, now cricket's cancelled,
this isn't what he wanted!

He hangs his head and drops his lip,
he's feeling really moody.
Disappointment makes him sulk,
his shoulders slumped and droopy.

This feeling reminds Angus
of what he really cares about,
and it's easier for him to cope
the next time things don't work out.

It's okay to feel disappointed
when everything goes wrong.
It helps to keep distracted
with a happy singalong.

When Harlow is feeling confident
she holds her head up high.
She's practised and she's capable,
her heart is full of pride.

Harlow can deal with the challenges
that come along each day.
She knows she'll bounce right back
when she makes her next mistake.

She stands up tall,
and speaks her mind,
Harlow knows that she can do it.

And when she fails, she tries again.

"There's really nothing to it!"

Tom feels embarrassed,
he wants to run and hide.
His cheeks are hot and flushed bright pink,
and shame fills up his mind.

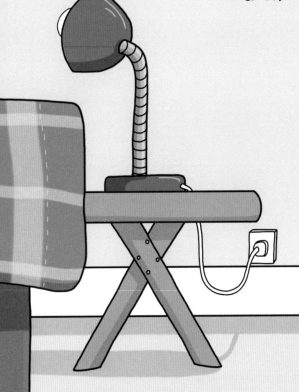

He thinks of all the silly things
that he's ever done . . .

. . . like the time he accidentally wore his trousers back to front!

But everybody makes mistakes,
it's okay to get things wrong.
Remember that your family
will love you all along.

Ayla feels insecure,
she's trying something new.

She hides behind her mummy's legs,
her cheeks get rosy too.
Her mind is very worried,
her tummy's full of butterflies.
But even though it's scary,
she knows it's worth a try.

This feeling lets Ayla know that she needs a helping hand.
It's true that sometimes new things don't go quite as we planned.
Ayla finds that over time her doubts get less and less.

"You know, it's true," says Ayla, "that practice makes progress!"

Lucas feels so jealous
when he sees his brother's toy,
or his sister gets attention . . .
she's stealing all the joy!

Jealousy makes Lucas frown,
his chest is tight and sticky.
He folds his arms across his front,
his tummy's feeling icky.

Feeling jealous lets Lucas know
that he really really cares.
It's useful to remember that
it's not helpful to compare.

Lucas knows that he's cared for
as much as his sister and brother.
It isn't 'things' that matter,
it's our love for one another.

Gracie's feeling silly,
she's having so much fun!
She laughs and plays, she dresses up . . .

and then pokes out her tongue!

She jumps, she spins,
she hangs, she twirls,
and then she runs around.

She cartwheels round the soft green lawn,
she just can't settle down.

Feeling silly now and then
releases stress and strife.
It helps to have a little fun
to weather storms in life.

Bella's heart feels guilty,
she knows that she's done wrong.
She's broken her mum's favourite vase
and her homework isn't done.

Bella bows her head,
her shoulders slump down heavy.
Guilt tells Bella to make things right . . .
"Say sorry when you're ready."

Guilt can teach us how to act
when we don't feel good inside.
It tells us we have hurt someone,
or that we've told a lie.

Bella feels a whole lot better
when she works to put things right.
She fixes up what went awry,
and now her heart feels light.

Feelings are messages from the heart
sent here to help you.

So listen close and take a breath,
they'll show you what to do.

All emotions come and go,
like weather and the clouds.
Let them be,
watch them pass,
all feelings are allowed.

WELCOME PARENTS, TEACHERS AND OTHER BIG PEOPLE — THIS SECTION IS FOR YOU!

On these pages you will find some wonderful tools and resources to help you to dive deeper into those Big Feelings! In this section you will learn some strategies to manage and explore emotions with your little one.

While it is wonderful to have a toolkit of techniques to teach children how to manage big feelings, remember this too: it is okay to simply just allow emotions to be. We don't always have to 'fix' feelings. And we certainly don't have to hurry them along or try to get rid of them for our children.

With this in mind, we can now arm ourselves, as the big people in their lives, with knowledge and understanding and walk alongside them as teachers, role models and mentors in the journey that is Big Feelings.

When children name and identify how they feel, it helps to 'down-regulate the limbic system' (that's the emotional centre of the brain). What does that mean? It means that when you expand your children's emotional vocabulary and help them to recognise *how* they feel, they are then able to better cope with those feelings and to calm themselves.

Big Feelings explores 14 different emotions experienced by 14 different characters. Each emotion is described in terms of both how it might make your little one feel, think or act, as well as how these emotions might either *help them* or how *they* can help themselves to navigate them.

Some ways you could use this book

Depending on the age or attention span of your little person, you might like to read through the whole story, or perhaps you might pick out just a few emotions to explore. Another useful idea is to read about the emotion they are experiencing or struggling with in a given moment, then perhaps experiment with some of the tools in this section to help them manage that emotion.

Ahead you'll find a smorgasbord of tools and resources to help you help your little one learn about and manage their big feelings.

Lets start with some questions to help you further explore their emotions, a big list of ideas to use when helping children to manage those very big feelings of theirs, and a range of 'distress tolerance' skills to teach and try.

Questions to further explore emotions with your children

Pick an emotion from this book and put it in place with these great conversation starters:

1. What makes you feel _____?

2. Where do you feel _____ in your body?

3. What do you think about when you feel _____?

4. How do you act when you feel _____?

5. What helps you when you feel _____?

6. What do you do to feel better again when you feel _____?

7. Who can help you when you feel _____?

Ideas to help children manage emotions

1. Name emotions out loud. This 'down-regulates' the emotional centre in their brains, helping them to process and cope with the feeling. Hint: this is helpful for us adults too!
   'It looks like you're feeling really angry' or 'I'm wondering if you're feeling worried right now?'

2. Validate their feelings.
   'It's okay to feel sad' or 'It's normal to feel scared when you're trying something new.'

3. Empathise.
   'It must be so tough when things don't work out how you wanted.'

4. Offer solutions and strategies or a listening ear or a hug.
   'Let's think of some ways you could overcome this fear' or 'Do you need a big squeezy hug?'

5. Allow each feeling to run its course — we don't have to 'fix' children's feelings.

6. Talk it through later if they are dysregulated (unable to manage emotions) in the moment. Kids can't access their logical brains when they are hijacked by big feelings, so the middle of a tantrum is not the time for adults to ask children to explain what's going on or try to talk them through a lesson about the feeling.
   'You were feeling so mad earlier; let's talk about what happened and how we could deal with it differently next time to keep you and others safe.'

7. Teach and practise the coping strategies in the following pages when kids are calm. This lays the foundations and forms solid pathways in the brain. This way, when kids are in the middle of their big feelings they have already learnt and practised the strategies they need in order to calm down again. We can't teach these things in the middle of their dysregulation.

8. Stay calm — big feelings in kids can throw us adults off-kilter too! Co-regulation is all about modelling calm and control to help our kids do the same.

9. Don't minimise their feelings — i.e. don't say: 'Oh there's nothing to be upset about, get over it.'

10. Share examples of your own experience of this emotion and how you cope:
    'When I'm feeling insecure I think about all the things in life that I thought I could never do, and now I can do well because I practised, like reading or riding a bike.'

11. Share (but don't compare) your feelings:
    'Mummy is feeling a bit sad today, and that's okay. I'm going to go for a walk to feel better. Would you like to come?' This models to children ways *they* might cope when *they* feel sad, while teaching them we, as adults, are okay with feeling our feelings, and that it isn't their job, as children, to fix those feelings for us.

12. Follow their lead — sometimes they want to talk, sometimes they just want to know you're there for a hug when they need it.

13. Remind them they are loved.

14. Take a mindful approach: name the emotion, accept that it is there, allow it to be there and watch it pass by when it is ready.

HOT CHOCOLATE BREATH

1. Hold your hands out in front of you and imagine you are holding a warm mug of hot chocolate.

2. Inhale slowly through your nose, imagining you are smelling the lovely hot chocolate aroma.

3. Exhale slowly through your lips as though you were trying to cool down the hot chocolate before you take a sip.

4. Repeat until you feel calm. You might even feel like your hands are warm, relaxed and cosy!

HAPPY PLACE

1. Close your eyes and take a few slow, deep breaths.

2. Imagine a place in your mind that makes you feel safe, happy and calm.

3. Think about all the little details — look around the space in your mind. What can you see? What can you hear? What can you smell? What can you reach out and touch?

You can come back to this safe and happy place in your mind whenever you are feeling sad, angry or worried.

COUNT TO 10

A great way to calm down when you are angry, anxious or afraid!

Pause where you are and slowly count to 10.

You could count each number in your mind and time it with a nice slow inhale.

3 GRATITUDES

Think about 3 things in your life that you are grateful for.

You could write these down on a list and add to it whenever you like.

You might think about people, places, things or activities that make you feel happy and content.

Thinking about the things that make you feel joy can help when you are feeling sad or insecure.

BELLY BREATH

This is a lovely technique to help calm and relax your body and mind.

Lie down and get comfortable. Place a book, teddy or pillow on your tummy.

Now, take deep, slow breaths right down into your belly.

Try to make the book rise and fall as your belly expands and deflates with each breath.

WORRY JAR

Create a worry jar to help manage stress, anxiety and worries.

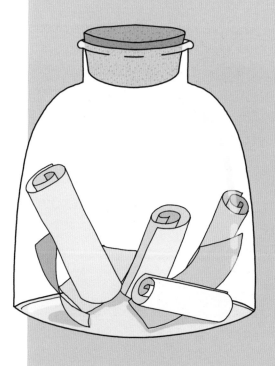

1. Take a jar and some pieces of paper.

2. Any time your mind feels full of worries, write them down on the bits of paper.

3. Put your worries into the jar.

4. Close the lid.

You can imagine that the jar is holding these worries for you and looking after them.

Now you don't have to hold on to them in your mind.

STAR JUMPS

Stand with your arms by your sides and your legs together, then jump both feet apart and bring your arms up above your head. Jump your feet back together again and bring your arms back down by your sides. Now keep going!

Star jumps help your body to cope with anxiety, frustration and anger!

WALL PUSH

If you're feeling angry, you can help let the feeling out safely by pushing as hard as you can against a wall.

This will help your body get rid of all that tension and deal with your anger in a safe way without hurting yourself or others around you.

SWAY BREATHING

Stand up tall. Now put your arms and legs out and sway off to one side, balancing on one foot. As you do this, take a long slow inhale.

Now slowly exhale as you lean back to the centre then over to the other side.

Repeat this action, inhaling and exhaling in time as you slowly sway side to side like a tree in the wind.

GIVE YOURSELF A HUG

When you're feeling sad or scared, sometimes a big squeezy hug is just the thing you need.

If there is no one around to give you a cuddle, or you'd like to try and make yourself feel better, you can give yourself a hug.

Just wrap your arms around your shoulders and squeeze tight!

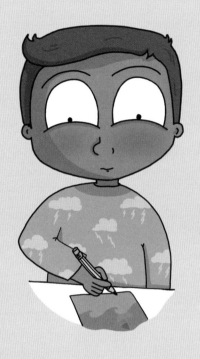

DRAW YOUR EMOTIONS

Imagine the feeling you are experiencing right now is sitting in front of you. I wonder what it would look like?

As you are drawing think about:

What does your feeling look like to you? e.g. is it a volcano? Is it a spiky hedgehog? Is it a rain cloud? Is it a bouncing ball?

How big would it be?

What colour is your emotion?

5 4 3 2 1

The perfect grounding technique to calm and refocus you in times of worry, fear and insecurity.

Look around you and spot FIVE things you can see — maybe describe them to yourself or look for things you hadn't noticed before.

Notice FOUR things that you can feel — you can reach out and touch different objects and textures.

Close your eyes and name THREE things you can hear.

List TWO things you can smell — move around to find something if you need to.

What is ONE thing you can taste? Or, if you can't taste anything right now, what is ONE thing you like about yourself?

FEELINGS THERMOMETERS

Teaching children to name their emotions out loud helps their brain to understand, process and cope with those feelings.

Once you have named the feeling, you can use 'feelings thermometers' to scale how big or small that emotion is.

When you know how strong a feeling is, it helps both adults and children to put in place a plan for how to manage it.

How to use these feelings thermometers

Kids can point to a mark on the feelings thermometers to show you how big their feeling is.

- If sadness is high, you'll need lots of self-care or support from an adult or friend.
- If confidence is low, you'll need to remind yourself of all the things you're good at and have achieved, and lean on others to help boost you up.
- If worry is high, you might need to do calming exercises (like hot chocolate breath or the worry jar), or try problem solving your worry with an adult you trust.
- If there is a little bit of anger, a few deep breaths might be enough. If there is a lot of anger, maybe some wall pushes, star jumps and counting to 10 might help.

Scaling emotions also teaches children that feelings ebb and flow; they change over time.

1. Ask your little one to rate how they are feeling on the thermometer. They might rate anger or anxiety as high, for example.
2. Now try out a few different calming and soothing strategies from this book.
3. Then ask your child to re-rate their emotion. Maybe now the emotion has lessened and they rate anger or anxiety as low.

This shows children they have the power to influence their emotions, and that feelings come and go.

HAPPINESS

ANGER

SADNESS

WORRY

SILLINESS

CONFIDENCE

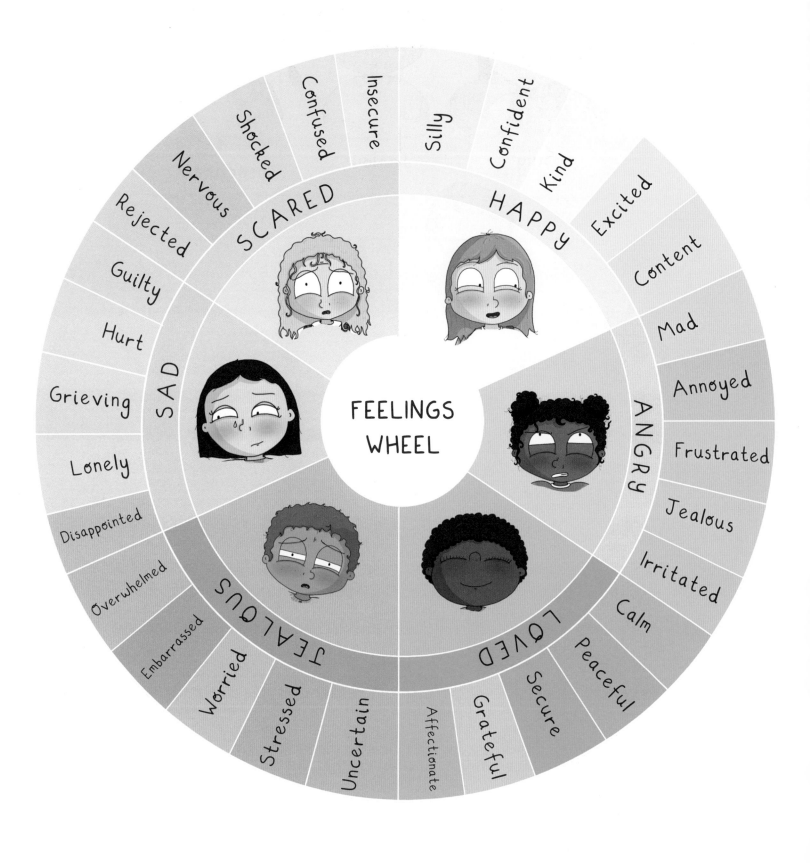

Silly

Jealous

Insecure

Scared

Disappointed

Confident

Embarrassed

Kind

Guilty

Angry

Anxious

Happy

Sad

Content

First published in 2022
Text and illustrations ©Rebekah Ballagh, 2022

All rights reserved. No part of this book may be reproduced or transmitted in any form or by any means, electronic or mechanical, including photocopying, recording or by any information storage and retrieval system, without prior permission in writing from the publisher.

Allen & Unwin
Level 2, 10 College Hill
Auckland 1011, New Zealand
Phone: (64 9) 377 3800

Email: info@allenandunwin.com
Web: www.allenandunwin.co.nz

83 Alexander Street
Crows Nest NSW 2065, Australia
Phone: (61 2) 8425 0100

A catalogue record for this book is available from the National Library of New Zealand

ISBN 978 1 99100 600 4

Design by Kate Barraclough
Printed and bound in China by
Hang Tai Printing Company Limited

10 9 8 7 6 5 4 3 2 1

FSC
www.fsc.org
MIX
Paper from
responsible sources
FSC® C023121